LIFE IN
FRESHWATER
Lakes

BY MIRELLA S. MILLER

Published by The Child's World®
1980 Lookout Drive • Mankato, MN 56003-1705
800-599-READ • www.childsworld.com

Acknowledgments
The Child's World®: Mary Berendes, Publishing Director
Red Line Editorial: Editorial direction
The Design Lab: Design
Amnet: Production

Design Elements: Shutterstock Images

Photographs ©: Shutterstock Images, cover (center), cover
(left), cover (top), cover (right), 6, 13, 17, 18, 21, 21 (top),
21 (middle left), 21 (middle right), 21 (right); Igor Kovalenko/
Shutterstock Images, 4–5; Pierre Leclerc/Shutterstock Images, 9;
Krzysztof Odziomek/Shutterstock Images, 10–11; Joseph M.
Arseneau/Shutterstock Images, 14

ISBN 9781626872950
LCCN 2014930649

Printed in the United States of America
Mankato, MN
July, 2014
PA02218

ABOUT THE AUTHOR

*Mirella S. Miller is a
writer and editor who lives
in Minnesota, the land of
10,000 lakes! One of her
favorite places to spend time is
at her grandparents' lake cabin
with her family.*

CONTENTS

Welcome to a Lake 4

What Is a Lake? 6

A Lake Forms 8

Lake Levels 10

The Shoreline 12

Open Water 14

Lake Trout 16

The Dark Deep 18

The Lake Food Chain 20

Glossary 22

To Learn More 23

Index 24

Welcome to a Lake

It is an early summer morning at the lake. The sun shines on the water. Small waves hit the shoreline. Frogs hop from one lily pad to the next. An eagle dives toward the water and catches a fish.

A snail darts across the muddy bottom of the lake.

This freshwater lake is a water biome. A biome is a place in nature that supports certain types of life. Plants and animals of a biome are specially suited to live there. Let's explore the freshwater lake biome!

Lakes provide plenty of food for hungry eagles.

What Is a Lake?

A lake is a deep body of water. Most lakes contain freshwater. This means the water is not salty. Lakes are

Lake Tahoe in Nevada has an area of 193 square miles (500 sq km).

found around the world. But about 70 percent of the world's lakes are in North America, Africa, and Asia.

Canada is home to almost half of the world's lakes.

Lakes can be big or small. Bigger lakes have waves, while smaller lakes are still. Lake Superior is the largest freshwater lake in the world. It borders the United States and Canada. Lake Superior's shoreline is 1,826 miles (2,939 km) long.

Sunlight cannot reach the deepest parts of a lake. Plants do not grow when there is no sun. The bottom of a lake has no plants.

Lakes usually connect to rivers or streams. Some rivers start at lakes. Other rivers end in lakes. The Niagara River empties into Lake Ontario. Both bodies of water border Ontario, Canada, and the state of New York.

Russia's Lake Baikal is the deepest lake in the world. It reaches a depth of 5,315 feet (1,620 m)!

A Lake Forms

There are many ways lakes form. The earth is always moving and shifting. This movement causes earthquakes. The ground shifts and produces **basins**. Over time the basins fill with water to become lakes. Many lakes in the western United States formed from earthquakes.

Other lakes form in the craters of **extinct** volcanoes. Crater Lake in Oregon filled when Mount Mazama caved in. Lakes also form in craters left behind by **meteorites**. These lakes are usually perfectly round.

New Quebec Crater in Canada formed after a meteor crashed into the land. This happened about 1.4 million years ago.

Glaciers produced most lakes in the Northern **Hemisphere**. Thousands of years ago, the earth

The five Great Lakes have a total surface area of 94,250 square miles (244,106 sq km). That is bigger than the United Kingdom!

went through different ice ages. Glaciers slid back and forth across the land. This made giant holes. Over time the holes filled with water from melted ice and rain to become lakes. Glaciers carved out the Great Lakes in the United States.

Crater Lake in Oregon is part of a U.S. National Park.

Lake Levels

Lakes have different levels. The levels are based on temperature. The water temperature is different for each level. The temperature also changes with the seasons.

The top level is warmest during the summer. Sunlight heats this level, but not the lower levels. They are much colder. Plants grow in the top level. Many animals live there, too.

Fall brings fewer daylight hours and colder nights. The lake cools down. The wind mixes

Animals and plants adjust to changing temperatures in a lake.

the water levels together. The levels have similar temperatures.

Some lakes are covered with ice during the winter. The top level is the coldest. The ice blocks wind from mixing the water. It also stops heat from escaping. This means the bottom is the warmest level. Many animals **hibernate** at the bottom of a lake during winter.

The ice melts in the spring. The wind mixes the water together again. Animals and food move through all levels of lakes.

The Shoreline

Lakes have three **zones**. They are the shoreline, open water, and bottom. Different plants and animals live in each zone. The shoreline is the area along the edge of a lake. It has the most variety of plants and animals.

A lakeshore's damp soil helps trees grow. The white bark of birch trees line many shores. Tall cottonwood and shady willow trees also grow.

The water is not deep near the shoreline. Sun easily reaches the bottom where plants can grow. You can find tall grasses and floating lilies. Deer and moose visit lakes for water and food. They like to eat water plants. Dragonflies make their homes in the tall grasses. So do many birds. Frogs sit on water lilies and catch flies. Small fish hide under the lily pads. Snails and crayfish crawl on the lake bottom.

A moose eats grasses near a lakeshore in Denali National Park.

Open Water

The open water is the top part of a lake. It receives the most sunlight. The shoreline surrounds the open water.

A green bullfrog hides in a lake's duckweed.

Photosynthesis happens the most near the top of the lake. This is the process plants use to make energy from sunlight. Animals then eat these plants. The animals absorb a plant's energy.

In open water, animals and plants move with the water. Plants float on the water's surface. One of these plants is duckweed. This is a small green plant with one root. It is a home for **plankton**. It is also food for ducks.

Many open water animals eat plankton and algae. Painted turtles and fish feed on the tiny plants and creatures. Many types of freshwater fish live in lakes. Lake Superior has 55 different kinds of fish. Some common kinds are perch, bass, salmon, and pike. Bigger animals and birds feed on fish. Loons and eagles dive into the open water to hunt for food.

Lake Trout

Lake trout are freshwater fish found in North American lakes. Lake trout eggs hatch in early spring. The fish are born in shallow water. As they grow, lake trout live in cold, deep water.

Lake trout can grow very big for fish. The average weight is 6.6 pounds (3 kg). But lake trout can weigh more than 59 pounds (27 kg). This fish has spots on its head, back, and fins. This makes it easy to point out a lake trout. A trout's V-shaped back fin is split. This helps lake trout swim fast.

Lake trout can live more than 25 years!

Being able to swim fast helps lake trout catch its food. A trout's **prey** includes shrimp, insects, plankton, and other fish. These other fish eat young lake trout. Adult lake trout have few

*Brown trout live in freshwater lakes and
other bodies of water.*

predators since they live in deep water. Sea
lampreys are the trout's main predator. Humans
also fish for trout.

The Dark Deep

The bottom of the lake is the last zone. It is the deepest and the darkest. No sunlight can reach this level. During the summer it is the coldest zone. Few plants or animals live in this zone. There is little **oxygen** at the bottom of the lake.

A marbled crayfish holds its babies under its tail.

Algae and other **organisms** live at the bottom. They break down matter around them. This matter then becomes food for other animals.

Worms also help make food. They move the soil around, too. This helps keep the lake healthy. Worms dig into the mud to hide from crayfish. Crayfish use their claws to look for worms. They also attack other animals.

The most common fish at the bottom of lakes is the bullhead. It is a type of catfish. Bullhead fish eat anything, including crayfish. Bullheads use fins to find food in a lake's muddy bottom.

The Lake Food Chain

Many plants and animals live in lakes. Each is an important part of a lake's food chain. This is the way that plants and animals work together in a habitat.

A lake food chain starts with the sun. The sun helps plants grow. Small animals, like plankton, eat these plants. Insects feed on plankton and other small animals. Insects then become food for fish, birds, and reptiles. Large animals feed on the smaller animals. Bacteria, fungus, and worms break down dead matter. This keeps a lake healthy for all plants and animals.

Every part of a freshwater lake food chain is very important. Its plants and animals work together to create a healthy habitat. Without one plant or animal, a lake biome would not be the same. A freshwater lake biome is an important part of nature.

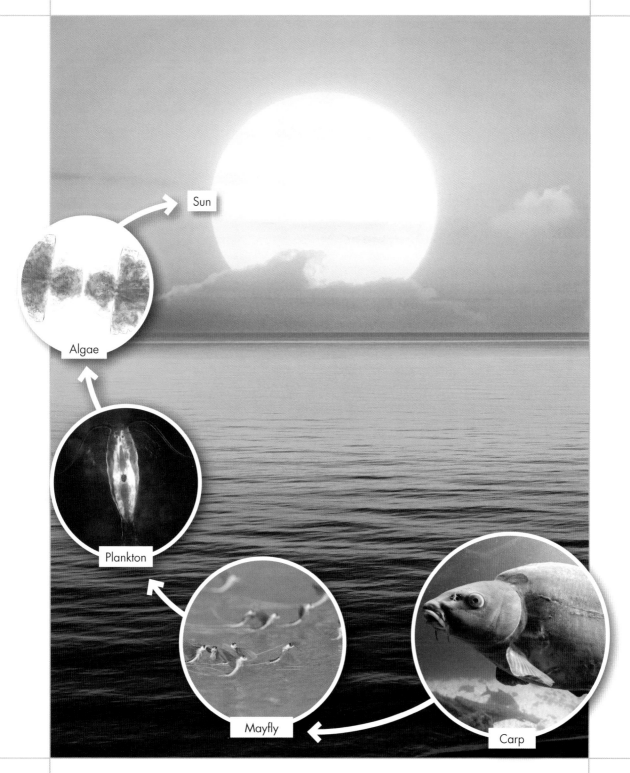

Sun

Algae

Plankton

Mayfly

Carp

In one kind of lake food chain, fish eat insects, insects eat plankton, plankton eat algae, and algae use the sun's energy to grow.

GLOSSARY

basins (BAY-suhns) Basins are large or small hollow areas in the surface of the land. Basins fill with water to become lakes.

extinct (ek-STINGKT) Something that is extinct is no longer active. Some lakes form from extinct volcanoes.

hemisphere (HEM-uhss-fihr) A hemisphere is one half of the earth divided by the equator. Glaciers produced most lakes in Earth's Northern Hemisphere.

hibernate (HYE-bur-nate) To hibernate is to pass the winter in a deep sleep. Many lake animals hibernate during the winter.

meteorites (MEE-tee-ur-rites) Meteorites are parts of meteors that reach the surface of the earth. Meteorites create caters that form into lakes.

organisms (OR-guh-niz-uhmz) Organisms are living plants and animals. Algae are organisms.

oxygen (OK-suh-juhn) Oxygen is an element found in rocks and water that is colorless, tasteless, and odorless. There is less oxygen in the water near a lake's bottom.

photosynthesis (foh-toh-SIN-thi-sis) Photosynthesis is the process plants use to convert sunlight into food energy. Plants use photosynthesis to grow.

plankton (PLANGK-ton) Plankton are tiny plants and animals that drift in water. Plankton live under duckweed.

predators (PRED-uh-turz) Predators are animals that hunt other animals for food. Adult trout have few predators in a lake.

prey (PRAY) Prey are animals that are hunted for food by other animals. Fish are prey for lake trout.

zones (ZOHNS) Zones are areas set off from surrounding parts. Lakes have three zones.

TO LEARN MORE

BOOKS

Aloian, Molly and Bobbie Kalman. *Water Habitats*. New York: Crabtree Publishing, 2007.

Crewe, Sabrina. *In Rivers, Lakes, and Ponds*. New York: Chelsea Clubhouse, 2010.

Kummer, Patricia K. *The Great Lakes*. New York: Marshall Cavendish, 2008.

WEB SITES

Visit our Web site for links about the freshwater lake biome:
childsworld.com/links

Note to Parents, Teachers, and Librarians: We routinely verify our Web links to make sure they are safe and active sites. So encourage your readers to check them out!

INDEX

basins, 8
bullhead fish, 19

Crater Lake, 8

duckweed, 15

extinct volcanoes, 8

glaciers, 8–9
Great Lakes, 8, 9

Lake Baikal, 7
lake bottom, 11, 12, 18–19
lake food chain, 20-21
lake levels, 10–11

Lake Ontario, 7
Lake Superior, 7, 15
Lake trout, 16–17

Mount Mazama, 8

New Quebec Crater, 8
Niagara River, 7
Northern Hemisphere, 8

open water, 14–15

painted turtles, 15
plankton, 15, 16, 20

shoreline, 4, 7, 12, 14